ANDY GUZZE[...]

Coaching Up

FROM
High School Football
TO Wall Street

outskirts
press

Coaching Up
From High School Football to Wall Street
All Rights Reserved.
Copyright © 2019 Andy Guzzetti
v2.0

The opinions expressed in this manuscript are solely the opinions of the author and do not represent the opinions or thoughts of the publisher. The author has represented and warranted full ownership and/or legal right to publish all the materials in this book.

This book may not be reproduced, transmitted, or stored in whole or in part by any means, including graphic, electronic, or mechanical without the express written consent of the publisher except in the case of brief quotations embodied in critical articles and reviews.

Outskirts Press, Inc.
http://www.outskirtspress.com

Paperback ISBN: 978-1-9772-1085-2
Hardback ISBN: 978-1-9772-1090-6

Cover Photo © 2019 Andy Guzzetti. All rights reserved - used with permission.

Outskirts Press and the "OP" logo are trademarks belonging to Outskirts Press, Inc.

PRINTED IN THE UNITED STATES OF AMERICA

Table of Contents

Foreword i
1. Developing a "Must Prospecting Discipline" 1
2. Gap Builders 8
3. Rank Your Office and See the Competition Begin 14
4. Protecting the Downside 21
5. 10 Principles of Investing 25
6. Advisory Account Quarterly Performance Reports:
   Advisors & Investors Must Use Them 34
7. Leadership 38
8. A New Mandate for Financial Advisors 51
9. Another Warning "Nobody Loses" 58

Foreword

The idea to write this book originated at the Plaza Hotel in NYC in the late '90s when I was addressing 500 new advisors in the business for one or two years. These newly minted advisors worked for the large wire house with which I was associated and traveled from all over the country to attend this award meeting in NYC. The meeting was held to recognize those new advisors who were tops in their classes. I remember standing on the stage, never behind a podium, congratulating the attendees, sharing with them my thoughts about becoming "superstar advisors" and how we needed their help to build great offices that would help clients meet their financial goals and objectives.

About halfway through the presentation I started to think about my coaching roots and how the same concepts and ideas I used at Proctor High School in Utica, New York to lead high school football players, to build teams, or to have a successful algebra class were the same concepts and ideas I was sharing with these successful young advisors. The only difference was the fact that I was being compensated fifty times more. This realization happened a few other times. I was invited every quarter to give a presentation to all the new managers and sales managers at the wire house training center in Hartford, Connecticut. The title of my presentation was "Coaching Financial Consultants and Building Great Offices." Almost every time I walked into the classroom at the training center I pictured the locker rooms at Proctor High School. I have learned much in the years since my

i

coaching days. I left Proctor High School to become the defensive coordinator at Hamilton College and also the head baseball coach. I left education and coaching in 1983 and started my successful career as a financial consultant in the same year.

After five years I was asked to go to the national training center in Chicago, Illinois, where I spent two years helping to train thousands of new advisors. During my period at the training center I spent a great deal of time not only training the new advisors but going on the road to "coach up" experienced advisors and managers. These were great opportunities to coach and learn before I became a branch manager. I have led offices in Sarasota, Florida, Clearwater, Florida, New York City, and Albany, New York–always using the ideas expressed in this book. As you read, please understand that these concepts I discuss can be used by anyone who wants to help others succeed, build a team, manage an office or lead a corporation.

This book probably would have been written sooner if not for the prosecutorial overreach of the SEC. I only mention this to warn all advisors and managers to protect your franchise, which means to protect your licenses. I settled the issue recently, five years later and $500,000+ poorer. I agreed to neither admit or deny and paid a $20,000 fine. The administrative law judge was ruled unconstitutionally appointed by the Supreme Court and the SEC gave me the choice of retrial or settling. My choice was spending another $500,000+ and arguing my case against an overreaching enforcement arm of the SEC, in front of an in-house administrative law judge who gave me the impression that I was guilty until proven innocent. I am not going to spend time relitigating the case but take this as a warning, YOU DON'T HAVE A CHANCE to win in front of an SEC Administrative Law Judge. Here is an example to prove my point. This was reported in the Wall Street Journal 11/22/15 about the beginning of my trial...... "In a small, windowless courtroom in downtown Manhattan, the chief in-house judge for the Securities and Exchange Commission told eight stockbrokers to give up on the idea that she would toss the case against them without first holding a hearing. Clad in a black robe, Judge Brenda Murray explained to the brokers that the commissioners who run the SEC and approve all the civil charges filed by the agency don't want its judges second-guessing them. "So for me to say I am wiping it out," Ms. Murray said at the hearing last year, "it looks like I am saying to these presidential appointed commissioners, I am reversing you. And they don't like that." The incident, disclosed in a court filing that hasn't been previously reported, helps illuminate the concerns of defendants who worry that they can't get a fair hearing in an internal court system where the SEC wins more often than it does in federal court." I repeat PROTECT YOUR FRANCHISE. Be proactive.

CHAPTER 1

Developing a "Must Prospecting Discipline"

Great business leaders have always had strong beliefs about their businesses. Having strong beliefs helps make the very difficult decisions seem a little less difficult. Great business leaders make decisions quickly and change them, if ever, slowly. The average person does the opposite. I have tried to make the following formula the backbone for all my decisions when it comes to the brokerage/advisory business, especially when assisting advisors to grow their business. A x V=G stands for A=assets under management, V= velocity at which we turn those assets over and G= gross production to advisor. Simply stated, the amount of assets we manage multiplied by the rate we charge equals our revenue. In today's advisory world, whether commission based or fee-based, we cannot raise G by increasing V. Competition, regulatory issues and fiduciary responsibilities make it impossible to depend on V for increased production. The only way to increase G is to increase A (assets under management). We can think about increasing fees (V), but in today's very competitive environment that can prove difficult. We can try to increase services offered such as charging for a financial plan or offering insurance products, we are really increasing assets under management (A). As a leader, using this formula helps you make decisions on the revenue side as well as the expenditure side. Hiring decisions become easier as it helps us focus on what skills we are looking for as we interview candidates.

If we are looking for someone to bring in assets, we are looking for relationship builders, great communicators --as opposed to stock market experts. Many great leaders recommend reading Dale Carnegie's 1936 seminal work on "How to Win Friends and Influence People." Warren Buffett took the Dale Carnegie course "How to Win Friends and Influence People" when he was twenty years old, and to this day he has the diploma in his office.

I have seen many advisors hired only because "they like the stock market" and have been successful investors. In 1988, while working with new trainees at a large wire house, we ran a study on what previous job experience the successful trainees came from. The results were very simple, there was no one job experience that correlated with successful advisors. The only business correlation we found was PhDs do not do well in the retail advisory business. A study of the Forbes 400 found there's actually an inverse relationship between the level of formal education and very wealthy people. Prospecting (and sales in general) requires humility and, yes, at times, eating crow. Formally educated people often have a sense of entitlement. As we are seeking to hire advisors who can "gather assets," I have found that our clients do not want to be sold an idea, they want to be educated. Yes — the bedrock of marketing is education. It has been my experience that teachers or coaches have the skills necessary to succeed. Again, our formula and our belief in the formula helps in hiring. As a manager in an advisory firm you are constantly bombarded with requests from advisors for dollars to spend on their businesses. Our formula reports the only question an advisor needs to answer when making a request for dollars: "How will this expenditure bring in more assets and how will you track results?" Training decisions are made easier as we help our advisors develop "A Must Prospecting Discipline." We can help advisors with product knowledge and market knowledge but

DEVELOPING A "MUST PROSPECTING DISCIPLINE"

our main focus is prospecting, prospecting, and prospecting. Making outbound calls, mailing correspondence to leads, holding seminars, teaching investment courses are just some of the areas that make up successful Must Prospecting Disciplines. Prospecting involves solicitation and rekindling leads that have cooled off. In other words, let's concentrate on process, not product.

If advisors want to consistently increase assets under management, they have to develop their own "Must Prospecting Discipline" which includes a referral generation system. This concept was an offshoot from an article I wrote in *Coach & Athlete* magazine in 1979 when I was a high school football coach. The article entitled "Developing a Must-Pass Play" was based on the desire to have a successful pass offense that we "must" run perfectly while the defense "must" work to stop it.

Successful advisors build their practices with strong "MUST" prospecting disciplines. Building a "MUST" prospecting discipline takes in many of the same characteristics as building a "MUST" pass offense. Again our "MUST" pass offense must be run perfectly and our defense must be able to stop it.

First, run the pass play out of our formations. When developing your "Must Prospecting Discipline" make sure you know what "formations" you are best at and what "formations are allowed at the firm where you are currently working. Cold calling, presenting seminars, networking, cold walking or social networking are some activities to think about. Let's look at some of these activities. Cold calling was at one time the only way to start building an advisory practice. Many have shied away from cold calling because of all the negative "boiler room" perceptions from investors and regulators. However, cold calling to me was not selling a product on a call but the ability to introduce yourself and your firm, qualify a prospect for their financial goals and objectives, and share an idea that fits the prospect's goals and objectives. In other sections we will go into details about the anatomy of sales. Our ultimate goal is to meet the prospect in our office or out of the office. No one is going to give significant assets to an advisor without sitting down with the advisor. There are restrictions (do not call lists) that regulators have set up and many advisors have used these increased regulations as an excuse to stay away from cold calling. Many advisors have resorted to cold-emailing, which has become what I believe to be a cop out from the uncomfortable task of initial contacts. In my opinion an introductory cold call, not a product-selling cold call, is still effective, especially since there is not much competition.

Seminars are another effective form of prospecting. Are you comfortable getting up in front of a group to sell your services? Seminars come with a cost: can you or your firm afford to do seminars? When mentioning the term "comfortable" please remember that successful advisors do the uncomfortable tasks that the unsuccessful won't do. Prospecting is uncomfortable (cold calling, cold walking, seminar presentations) to many advisors. When an advisor comes to me for assistance because they hit a plateau in their business development the first thing I ask is: "What prospecting activity makes you uncomfortable?" Once you identify that uncomfortable activity, you must work to become comfortable with that activity and your production will increase. Your network is your net worth — a prospecting list is a blueprint for success. People are the inventory. A great list of leads doesn't help sitting in a folder gathering computer dust or office dust.

The new advisors are uncomfortable with the entire prospecting scene, cold calling, etc. Experienced advisors usually hit the plateau because of the uncomfortable activity of "asking for referrals." They may say their new business comes from referrals but they really have no prospecting discipline to get referrals. It is uncomfortable; beat it and new business (assets) develops.

DEVELOPING A "MUST PROSPECTING DISCIPLINE"

Don't try to change your "formations" or your firm's "formations." Work to develop your "MUST" prospecting discipline within the formation you have.

Second, our personnel must have the skills to run our "Must Pass Play." We needed athletes that can run, catch the ball and throw the ball. In developing your Must Prospecting Discipline you must have the skills, or work to develop the skills necessary to enable your plan to succeed. The plan must fit you. Do you have the platform skills to give seminars? Here is where the term "uncomfortable" originates. Don't shy away from the activity that makes you uncomfortable--beat it. Many advisors avoid being the presenter by bringing in guest speakers (money managers, wholesalers etc.). It has been my experience that the speaker is the show and it helps you gather assets if you are the main focus of the seminar. One major downfall of seminars is the lack of follow up. You must call everyone on the list of attendees. Make sure you get a list of all attendees. Your goal is to get them in for an appointment. When I was managing a brokerage office in Sarasota, Florida seminars were great prospecting tools used by many advisors. However, some thought that seminars were costly and the effectiveness was spotty.

When I arrived at this branch I decided to attend all the seminars and track account openings and new assets. Two seminar presentations stand out as examples of follow-up. The first seminar was given about managed money by a very experienced advisor. The power point was excellent, the advisor had great platform skills and the content was very informative. The second seminar I attended was presented by a new advisor (one year in the business). It was a very general presentation about investing, the presentation skills were adequate and the power point was kind of busy (too much information to digest). I tracked the new account openings and new assets brought in from seminar attendees. The results surprised me at first. The new advisor opened up four times as many accounts as did the experienced advisor in the six-month period I tracked and brought in ten times as many new assets. Why? Follow up!! The experienced advisor waited for seminar attendees to call him. Why not? It was a well-presented seminar with a great deal of knowledge shared with the attendees. The junior advisor followed up with a phone call to invite them in for an appointment and didn't stop at one call. She knew that the success of her seminars depended on follow up. Seminars without follow-up do not work.

Do you have the skills to "cold call"? As I said before, we are not talking about product(stock) cold calling. We are using cold calling as an introductory call to our firm, ourselves, and the advantages of working with our group. It is very difficult to cold call on a consistent basis. The rejections make it tiresome. One program we have used successfully is called "10 before 10." Make it your goal to make ten cold calls daily before 10:00 am. This is not an onerous task and it gives you consistency. It allows you to get calls in before the tasks of the day take over. You, of course, can make more calls but make sure you hit your 10 before 10. The goal is to start with suspects, develop a prospect, and close a client.

Networking is another activity that can generate leads of possible clients. The major downfall of prospecting is failure to follow up. It does you no good to come back from a networking function with a pocket full of business cards and not follow up. Seminars without follow up don't work and networking without follow doesn't work.

Your "Must Prospecting Discipline" has to fit the skills you have and the skills you develop.

Third, our "Must Pass Play" must be ably executed in any type of weather. We cannot be stopped by rain, sleet or snow. The "weather" in the advisory business is the markets. Our prospecting discipline must work in all market conditions. We cannot hide in down mar-

DEVELOPING A "MUST PROSPECTING DISCIPLINE"

kets. In fact, a down market is a great time to prospect. Investors have questions about their current advisor, and many advisors hide during tough times.

Fourth, our "Must Pass Play" must attack the defenses we see. Demographics will dictate how and with what we attack the marketplace. When I was a manager in Florida we always gave the example that a "Must Prospecting Discipline" concentrating on commodities would not do well. Know your prospecting demographics, build your prospecting discipline around working with that group.

Fifth, practice so that you can run the "Must Pass Play" to perfection. You can't turn it on or turn it off haphazardly. Every day, every week, every month and every quarter must be used to perfect your prospecting skills. Know how to handle objections. Know your products. Whatever prospecting method you are using, use it and become an expert.

As a supervisor helping advisors develop successful "Must Prospecting Disciplines" that bring in a constant flow of new accounts and new assets will lessen compliance risk. There is nothing as dangerous as an advisor who has no prospecting discipline, can't see where his/her next trade will come from, and starts to depend on increasing V. An advisor who has a successful "Must Prospecting Discipline" concentrates on increasing A and is not worried about V.

CHAPTER 2

Gap Builders

Must show value through knowledge

What we know
↑
Gap builders establish | our value to investors
Perceived gap or knowledge | about potential investments
↓
What they know

"Price is an issue in the absence of value." The phrase is well known in the advisory industry and probably every industry. No client is going to pay an advisor a fee unless they perceive the advisor brings value. There must be a perceived gap of knowledge between client and advisor. The larger the perceived gap the less price becomes an issue. We talk a lot about "gap builders" because building that knowledge gap establishes an advisor's value to investors. Over the years many "gap builders" have not changed. In this chapter I will discuss a few areas that are important to investors and emphasize the fact that a lack of knowledge in these areas can hurt an investor. There are many topics that pop up that can help show the knowledge gap. The following are some topics that can always be used.

Fixed income investments (bonds) fluctuate in value

I have seen many investors who were very surprised when their bond mutual fund, even a government bond fund, declined in value. At this time I believe 75% of all investors do not know that bonds can fluctuate in value. Most investors assume that stocks are volatile but bonds are safe. If an advisor can explain to a client or a prospect how bonds can fluctuate in value they will begin exposing that knowledge gap. This gap filler is especially timely today as the fed raises interest rates and puts pressure on the value of bond portfolios. An advisor should make every effort to explain the fluctuation of bond values.

When I was managing a brokerage office in Sarasota, Florida for a large wire house we used to bring down our fixed income managers from NYC to discuss the bond market. Before we began the presentation I had to remind the managers about general comments on the bond markets. When bond managers say the coming year will be a good one, they believe interest rates will be going down (the value of their portfolios go up). The investors attending the presentation think a good year for bonds is when interest rates are going up. Their CDs and other fixed income investments will pay more. If an advisor explains the relationship to bond values and interest rates the advisor is bridging the knowledge gap that's been exposed. The client or prospect thinks "Wow, I didn't know that."

Growth manager vs. Value manager

I believe 85% of all investors do not know the difference between a growth manager and a value manager. Explaining the difference between a growth manager and a value manager is a great "gap builder."

A value manager looks for securities that are undervalued. The manager may look for low p/e ratios or low price to book ratios. Growth managers focus on companies that are still expanding and expected to generate increased revenue, rather than those that pay dividends. This discussion can lead into a discussion about mutual fund "overlap."

How many times have we seen a client who says they are diversified because they own ten mutual funds but when we check for "overlap," the stock holdings in these funds overlap to a point where the goal of diversification is not met. Because the client did not understand growth vs. value managing styles their portfolios were not what they thought they were. By explaining "growth vs. value" the advisor brings value to the relationship. Price is not an issue.

Taxable equivalent yield

How many times have we heard the phrase "it is not what you make; it is what you keep"? Many investors have heard the phrase but not many know how to figure out the differences between a taxable investment and a tax-free investment. Another great "gap builder." Example: if an investor purchases a tax-free municipal bond paying 4% what percentage rate on a taxable investment would equal the same money they keep? If the investor is in the 28% tax bracket the formula is .04/(1-.28)=.055(5.5%). The investor would have to get an interest rate of 5.5% (taxable equivalent yield) to end up keeping the same amount of money. Another great "gap builder" is created as an investor tries to decide on a taxable vs. tax-free investment and the advisor shows how to efficiently do the comparison.

Power of compounding

Investors are very concerned about knowing what their investments will be worth at a certain date in the future. Advisors can draw attention to the knowledge gap by discussing the power of compounding. As advisors we think that all investors know what we know—especially the concept of compounding. Advisors can fill the gaps by discussing the "rule of 72" or "the rule of 115." Just as a reminder, the rule of 72 can tell you when invested money will double by dividing 72 by the interest rate earned. Ex: interest rate is 8%. Dividing 72 by 8 will equal 9. In nine years your investment will double. The rule of 115 will tell you when an investment will triple. Ex: interest rate is 8%. Divide 115 by 8 will equal 14.375. In 14.375 your investment will triple. Discussing these numbers with a client will help bridge the knowledge gap. Another "gap builder" concerns compounding tax deferred (IRA, 401k, annuity). How many times has a client asked you "how much does your IRA pay"? For years banks have convinced investors that an IRA is an investment. An IRA is an account but, of course, bank IRA are just CDs put in an IRA. The banks have also convinced investors that the reduction in current taxes owed by taking of your contribution is important, and it is, but the most important and rewarding factor of an IRA is compounding tax deferred. Your money grows faster as you do not pay taxes on the earnings each year. You compound without paying taxes on the earnings. Seems simple but this explanation about qualified money vs. after tax investing can help fill that knowledge gap.

Current events

We are paid to have an opinion, especially when it comes to current events. Some areas that help create gaps are oil prices (gas), economy, new tax laws, real estate, and interest rates. A very new area that will help advisors expose the knowledge gap and bring value is the ability to interpret news, especially the "main street media (MSM)." It has become quite obvious, at least to me, that the reluctance of the main street media to correctly report the financial news in order to hurt President Trump makes it very difficult for investors to make well-thought-out decisions. Advisors must be able to give clients the facts without political bias. This has become another duty that advisors must undertake to protect investors. One example is how the main street media has latched onto the worry that Trump's tariff policies will create worldwide chaos. Anytime there is a blip in the stock market the headlines will shout out how "the worry about a trade war is causing investors to sell." Critics will use anything that blames Trump for negative economic occurrences. Helping to interpret the financial news peppered with political rhetoric is another great "gap builder" that clients perceive as value. We will discuss this new mandate for advisors later in the book.

Rebalance strategy

More and more advisors are advising clients about retirement savings. A knowledge gap using the phrase "sell high buy low" can easily be exposed. Normally most investors who want to make money in the equity markets have been told it is simple: "buy low, sell high." Investors become intrigued when we change the phrase. We believe in asset allocation, diversification and rebalancing especially when we are counseling clients on 401k investing. After choosing the correct asset allocation for a client to create diversification and meeting the client's risk tolerance, we must continually monitor the portfolio to make sure the percentages chosen are maintained. The monitoring can be scheduled yearly, quarterly or semi-annually. Example: a client decides to put 25% into four funds......25% large cap growth fund, 25% small cap growth fund, 25% international equity fund, and 25% in a fixed income fund. We decide to monitor on a yearly basis. After the first year the percentages have changed to 30% large cap growth, 23% small cap growth, 25% international, and 22% fixed income. How many investors would sell the winner and distribute the dollars into the two losers? To effectively rebalance a portfolio we have to sell the winners and buy the losers. Not many clients would do this on their own. We as advisors know that an asset class that out performs will not continue to do that on a consistent basis. This rebalancing will protect the investor from being over-allocated in an asset class when that asset class gets hit.

Gap builders are used to prove to clients, prospects and suspects that we bring value. Clients must believe that there is a significant gap between what you know and what they know, the larger the gap the more value you bring to the relationship.

CHAPTER 3

Rank Your Office and See the Competition Begin

Most offices/complexes in the financial services industry, whether it be RIAs or brokerage firms, are ranked formally or informally by gross production. The advisor who generates the most commissions is #1 and all others fall in line according to their gross production. This is a time- honored industry ranking system that doesn't help the advisors or the managers create a climate to cultivate competition in the areas that drive our business and ultimately create the rewards for clients and advisors. The Guzzetti ranking system prevents an advisor's business from becoming stagnant. By ranking an office, advisors know they are being evaluated. It will reveal weaknesses where it counts the most--prospecting for new clients and new assets. It is not uncommon for larger producers to get complacent, especially in the area of prospecting for new business. You will have some experienced advisors who do not like the system as younger advisors pass them in the rankings. To those advisors who are concerned, we just ask them to use the system to help evaluate their business. Am I prospecting enough, am I asking for referrals, am I growing my asset base? If not, why not? Nothing fails like success.

RANK YOUR OFFICE AND SEE THE COMPETITION BEGIN

We have used the "Guzzetti Ranking System" (GRS) in wire house offices and RIA offices. If one uses the GRS, the leaders/managers must first buy into a formula that we believe drives our business:

A x V=G (A) **Assets** we have under management **times** the
(V) **Velocity** with which we turn those assets over **equals** the
(G) **Gross** production.

In today's environment the emphasis has to be on (A) assets as (V) has been dramatically brought down through reduced commission and fee structures. If our goal is to increase our (G) gross production, we must concentrate our efforts on increasing (A) assets under management. GRS takes into account the activities that help increase our assets under management as well as results (G) gross production.

We normally rank an office quarterly using three categories:

1. New accounts opened
2. New assets brought in
3. Gross production.

This is a simple process, we will use an actual example of a 43-advisor office (rankings attached, names redacted). We rank the office in the three categories listed above.

Points are awarded as follows:

- if an advisor is ranked # 1 in new accounts opened, 43 points are awarded, #2 gets 42 pts and we go down the line. The same for new assets brought in and gross production. We now have 3 numbers for each advisor
- double the gross production number. In our 43 person office the #1 ranked in production gets 86 pts, #2 84 pts etc. why double the points earned in production category? First of

15

all, we value production and production should be rewarded. Secondly, for a growing advisor with a low ranking in production to show well in the rankings he/she must be performing well in the other two categories, new assets and new accounts. These are activities that must be rewarded.

- add the points up
  e.g. An advisor ranks #1 in gross production worth 43 pts (in the attached), #7 in new assets worth 37 pts and #11 in new accounts opened worth 33 pts. Double the gross production pts 43x2=86 + 37 pts new assets + 33 pts for new accounts opened. This advisor's point total is 156 pts.
- We calculate each advisor's point totals and then rank the office by the point totals. Ties go to the advisor with the higher gross production.
- When I initially instituted the system, I ran into one problem when ranking "new assets." An increase or decrease in assets could be affected by the results of the equity and bond markets. The increase or decrease in assets did not only reflect results of prospecting but showed the effect of markets. While attending a national managers' meeting I had the opportunity to discuss my ranking system with a group of managers and divisional directors. My concerns with the reporting system were quickly relayed to the folks who were in charge of generating reports and just as quickly they were able to generate a report that showed only new assets without market results. When that happened we had a perfect ranking system that reflected the correct results from activities we wanted to track.

These rankings are then distributed to all advisors (names included).

This system can help the advisor as well as the manager. The higher producing advisors can look to see if they are keeping up with their production ranking (which we also list on the quarterly rankings sheet). Since we double the point number for gross production, if a

RANK YOUR OFFICE AND SEE THE COMPETITION BEGIN

higher producing advisor falls down on the GRS, it means that he/she isn't bringing in new assets or opening up enough accounts and this is the only way of increasing an advisor's gross production.

As a manager/leader of an office, one of your responsibilities is to budget resources to help increase business. As advisors line up at your door to ask for financial assistance to do seminars, client appreciation dinners etc., this system helps you know where to allocate funds. In the old production ranking system, the top producers get the resources and we miss the "budding superstars" that deserve some resources. Take for instance, the #11 ranked advisor in the example; notice he/she is ranked #28 in gross production. It takes some great work in the areas of opening new accounts and increasing assets to move up the ranking system to #11. Remember we are doubling the points for gross production. This advisor deserves some financial assistance to help build their business. In the old production-driven ranking the #28 producers would not get many funds allocated to them. As you look at the attached ranking list, you can pick out the negatives and positives it shows. Some top producers aren't prospecting enough. Besides believing in the A x V=G formula for success, we also believe that it is imperative that all advisors have to develop a "MUST PROSPECTING SYSTEM." An advisor must continuously open new accounts and bring in new assets. All activities lead to increasing "A."

This ranking system also helps you justify your expense allocations. When an advisor comes into your office to complain about your allocation decisions, just take out the ranking results as a backup. I can remember the time a top producer came into my office to complain about some of my allocation decisions. This top producer had a very experienced four-person team that was doing over $1.5 million in production. He was disturbed that I had allocated funds to help a newer advisor do a seminar. He thought it was a waste of money that could have been used by his team. I used this opportunity to go back to the basic belief A x V=G. I took out the latest Guzzetti Ranking System report which had been passed out the previous week. I showed him the #8 ranked advisor who was #20 in production. That is the reason why I allocated funds to the #20 production advisor. He was performing the activities needed to build a successful practice.

I can share two exciting results from this one meeting. After the meeting with the "big" producer I was asked to attend his weekly team meeting to go into more detail about A x V=G and "Developing a Must Prospecting" discipline. The #8 ranking advisor who was central to this discussion is now a $3 million producer with a six-person team.

If you get your advisors to buy into the formula **A x V=G,** this ranking system gets the competition started and continues to reinforce the positive activities that lead to success in the advisory/brokerage profession. I am sure a group ranking system developed in any business or industry that tracks positive activities which increase revenue can be very helpful. We also help advisors develop their individual tracking programs to manage activities to improve their results. Outgoing calls are the lifeblood of opening new accounts and gathering assets. We have always tracked all daily outgoing calls. We put the results in our "Morning Notes" every day. Not everyone uses the numbers, but those who are building a practice know that these numbers can show how they are spending their time. Prospecting calls, appointments, phone presentations, service calls are some of the others we track.

When we discuss how an advisor is spending time, we work to develop everyone's "MUST PROSPECTING" discipline. If you have a "must prospecting" discipline it is very helpful to build a successful practice and move up the GUZZETTI RANKING SYSTEM.

RANK YOUR OFFICE AND SEE THE COMPETITION BEGIN

GUZZETTI RANKING SYSTEM (GRS)

RANK	ADVISOR	GROSS RANK	TOTAL SCORE
1		1	156
2		3	153
3		6	147
4		7	139
5		12	128
6		9	124
7		15	124
8		20	123
9		2	117
10		14	117
11		28	117
12		5	106
13		16	105
14		4	100
15		18	99
16		8	97
17		11	97
18		25	97
19		33	95
20		32	95
21		10	93
22		38	86
23		19	83
24		41	83
25		30	77
26		17	74
27		13	73
28		36	73
29		22	70

COACHING UP

30		40	69
31		39	67
32		24	64
33		26	63
34		34	62
35		21	61
36		29	61
37		23	56
38		37	50
39		27	46
40		31	45
41		43	39
42		42	24
43		35	20

CHAPTER **4**

Protecting the Downside

As advisors we are spending more time talking to clients about protecting assets rather than growing assets. Today's investor seems to be more worried about protecting the downside than capturing the upside. Many advisors spend most of their time explaining the upside potential of individual investments. Clients are only half listening because their minds are focused on the downside potential. One cannot avoid risk–only manage it. Advisors must address the "downside fears." We must address the risk in all investments. We have to be prepared to offer our clients the ability to handle the possibility of another 2007-2008. Many investors who saw their portfolios lose as much as 45% of value during the last major correction were not prepared for that possibility. Many of these investors bailed out of the markets at the lows and never got back in, missing this current bull market. The capital markets are self- cleansing. Markets don't crash; they correct.

Many investors have never heard about "tail risk" or "black swan." Now it has to be a part of every investor's vocabulary. What is 'tail risk," especially "left tail risk." If you look at the statistical bell-shaped curve below, we all know from our statistic classes that statistically 95% of all results fall in the curve. Money managers' hedge funds base most of their decisions on the curve. They are prepared to handle any event where results are inside the curve. What happens if results are in those little tails at each end? If it is on the right side, that would be positive; but the left side tail risk creates a negative problem. When these events happen the contagious effects take over, causing massive losses in different areas. When these things occur they are usually called "black swan" events. Everyone thought all swans were white and never expected to see a "black swan."

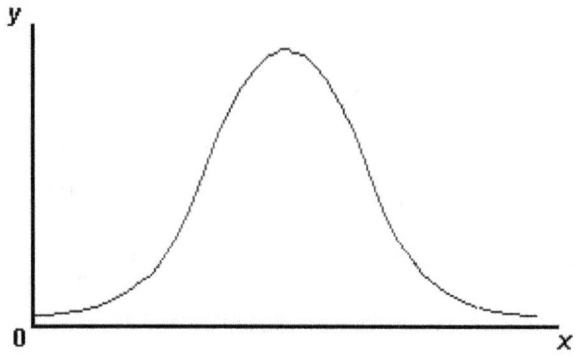

What are some solutions:

1. **VARIABLE ANNUITIES** can be used to protect investors in a number of ways. Two specific ways (there are approx. 1600 versions) that variable annuities can help protect the downside are:
    a. In a deferred variable annuity, negative returns are possible, but the industry has created various options to put investors at ease, such as riders that guarantee certain levels of income upon retirement. This guarantee of a certain income level has become a very key feature, especially for the retired or close to retirement baby boomers. Even if there is a "black swan event" your retirement income is guaranteed. In this era of companies getting away from defined benefit plans this guarantee allows investors to set up their own "defined benefit plan."

b. Guaranteed minimum death benefits can also protect the downside. Most deferred variable annuities sold include the basic kind: a guarantee that, if the account value has lost value when the investor dies, heirs will get the full amount initially invested. There are many variations of the minimum death benefit, such as "step ups" which are guarantees that heirs get the highest value the account hit on one of its anniversaries. According to the Insured Retirement Institute, between 2001 and 2003, variable annuity beneficiaries received $2.8 billion more than the account value when policyholders died earlier than expected.
2. **MANAGED FUTURES** can be used to protect the downside. Investors who want to be ready for a "Black Swan" event must have something in their portfolio that can make money not only on the upside but when values are falling. The values may be falling in equities, bonds or commodities and a managed futures program can make money in those falling markets, thus protecting some or all of your portfolio. The futures (commodity) markets have been built to hedge, although many investors try to speculate in these markets. The futures market is very complicated; that is why we do not recommend a "do it yourself" futures portfolio. Let the professional with a proven track record do it.
3. **DIVERSIFICATION/ASSET ALLOCATION** can be used to lessen downside risk. In the events we are discussing–especially in the last melt down–nothing was safe. However, diversification will protect you from being in one asset class that gets hammered.
4. **FDIC CDs/ MONEY MARKETS** can be used to protect the downside; however, with interest rates at record lows the returns may not even keep up with inflation. Having said that, we have all learned that cash is an asset class. Many investors forgot that fact and portfolios did not factor in cash while

building diversified portfolios. Nothing wrong with having a portion of your investment assets in cash.

Many advisors have other specific programs that can help with protecting the downside, including: covered call writing, married puts, and stop loss strategies to name a few. On a cautionary note, one investment that has caught on as a way to protect the downside is "target date funds." Target-date funds are taking over retirement accounts. According to a Vanguard report roughly half of retirement savers invested their entire account(401k) in a single target rate fund in 2017. In 2004 no one invested in a target-date fund. Vanguard estimates that the number will jump to 70% by 2022. Target-date funds are advertised as easy, one-investment retirement plans. Each fund holds a portfolio of stocks and bonds which is managed with a specific retirement date targeted. As the targeted retirement date approaches, the fund supposedly emphasizes caution, shifting more of its allocation to bonds. The investors think they are protecting their downside by "being more cautious" in bonds. As an example ,let's look at a target date 2020 fund which started with a 80/20 allocation to stocks and bonds and now, as we approach the 2020 target retirement date, the fund is allocated 20/80 stocks and bonds. Is there any advisor in their right mind who thinks that in today's interest rate environment a 20/80 allocation is protecting the downside? Today there is probably more risk in bonds than stocks. The fund families are pushing these funds to gather assets away from advisors (investors don't need your help). Target date funds do not protect the downside and I am not a fan. Investors need to individually determine their financial goals and their risk tolerance and then work with an advisor to come up with a program to 'help protect the downside.'

Advisors must talk about "downside risk." They can't just avoid it. Today, more than ever, investors are more concerned about protecting the downside than participating in the upside.

CHAPTER 5

10 Principles of Investing

There are many different choices that must be addressed when evaluating an investment opportunity. Will this investment opportunity make money, can I lose my money, can I get my money out if I need it? Sometimes potential investors can be overwhelmed with all of the information, leaving them confused and often frustrated. Mutual funds, separately managed accounts, individual bonds, annuities and other types of investments make the final decision difficult. They are bombarded with advertising, cold calls, and seminars from the financial services industry and often leave these experiences with more questions than answers.

The following 10 Principles can help all investors understand how to evaluate an investment opportunity. No matter what type of investment someone is looking at, these principles can be used to narrow the choices and help an investor ask the helpful questions. These principles pertain to both those individuals who are still accumulating their assets and those who are faced with the challenges of generating income from their assets after a lifetime of work. When I created this list, I was especially targeting retiring individuals or those who are getting close to retirement. Many individuals will be retiring with large sums in their 410k. These large amounts of dollars are targets for many advisors. To compound the decisions, many of these retirees have never invested outside their 401k and need help. We have used this "10 principles of investing" concept as the outline for many prospecting seminars.

Principle #1
Potential for Greater Return Means Potential for Greater Risk

When evaluating an investment opportunity, understanding this principle is a must. Terms like "safe" or "risky" are too vague and can often be quite misleading.

Investors should utilize this simple formula when determining whether or not an investment is appropriate for their portfolio.

> *(Anticipated Return on Investment) − (Ten-Year Treasury Interest Rate) = Additional Relative Risk*

> *For example, if the potential return on investment X = 10% and the current ten-year treasury is paying 5%, investors are assuming twice the risk in investment X as opposed to the ten-year treasury.*

Investors must ask themselves if they can accept that risk. As an investor you should know the level of risk involved in every investment and determine whether your portfolio can accept that risk.

Although this principle may sound straightforward it is very often overlooked by the lure of high double digit returns. The easiest example to show capital risk is portrayed when making a decision to chase yield, especially in the current low interest rate environment. An investor has a $100,000, 10-year very safe U.S. treasury bond that can be rolled over at 3%. A broker tells the investor about a high yield corporate bond mutual fund that is currently paying 7.5%. The increased rate of 7.5% can bring in an additional $4500/yr. The additional yield brings additional risk (high yield corporate bonds vs U.S. treasury). Can you accept that risk?

Principle #2
Every Investment Decision Involves Risk

Many investors define risk as the possibility of losing the principal put into an investment. While this is an example of a type of risk, it only illustrates the potential **Capital Risk**. There are other types of risk as well.

In fixed income investments there is **Interest Rate Risk**. If investors lock in an interest rate for a specific length of time and interest rates rise, the value of the investment can go down. Furthermore, if investors are locked into that investment they cannot take advantage of the higher rates. Everyone believes that a bank certificate of deposit is risk free because of FDIC insurance. There is no **capital risk** if held to maturity. But there is interest rate risk if an investor invests $100,000 in a 5yr CD with a 3% interest rate. If interest rates go up after two years and a 5 yr CD is now paying 5%, the investor cannot get out of the CD they are holding to invest in the new 5% CD unless they pay a penalty or there is a secondary market for the 3% CD. By not investing in the new rates the investor is losing $2,000/yr interest for the remaining 3yrs. If there is a secondary market and the investor wants to get out of the 3% CD, the potential for capital risk may be caused by the interest rate risk. In our example the investor decides they want to get out of their 5yr, 3% CD after 2yrs invested. A CD is a fixed income investment(bond). The investor will go out and get a bid (price) for their 5yr CD(now 3yrs). The price will be dictated by current interest rates for 3yr CDs. Let's say that the current rate for a 3yr CD is 4%. The investors' now $100,000 3yr CD is paying 3%. A buyer would offer less than the $100,000 originally invested, probably around $90,000. Interest rate risk can cause capital risk, especially in fixed income investments.

In addition, all investments are subject to **Inflation Risk**. Are your investment returns outpacing inflation rates? If not, you run the risk losing "buying power" and in effect are losing money. Current inflation rates at 2%/yr don't seem to present a risk but those investors who know what inflation rates were in the early '80s (10%+) can better understand inflation risk. Don't get lured into thinking inflation rates will remain at current low levels. If inflation rates increase, investors will have to make decisions that could increase risk to keep up with cost of goods we all need (cars, food, housing etc.)

Principle #3
There is No Free Lunch

Many investors and investment professionals alike focus on the "cost" of an investment. Debates between "load" and "no-load" mutual funds can sometimes cloud the picture when evaluating a particular mutual fund.

> *While cost is an important factor in determining the overall merit of an investment, decisions should never be based solely on cost. Investors limit their investment choices by basing their investment decisions on cost alone.*

It is important to realize how transaction costs and fees will cut into your overall returns and to weigh the investment opportunity accordingly.

There are always costs associated with your investments. The challenge is being able to know what those costs are and how they affect your return. We recently have witnessed the Department of Labor (DOL) trying to push through what is referred to as the DOL Fiduciary Rule. The false narrative was hammered into the discussions that fees and commissions cost the 401k (retirement accounts) investors $18 billion. The false narrative was used to push the bill along: "If there were no fees or commissions in retirement accounts, investors would have $18 billion more at retirement." The fees and commissions have bought advice that will protect investors from losing money. Who keeps investors from trying to time the markets? Most retail clients get in late and get out early unless they can rely on advice paid for with this $18 billion. If an investment manager charges more but returns more net fees than the competition, what investment would you want to have? Smart investors do their homework not only on cost but also on historical returns.

Principle #4
True Diversification Can Reduce Risk of Losing Principal

A truly diversified portfolio avoids being overly concentrated in any one asset class, recognizing that all asset classes have the potential to increase or decrease in value. Most individual investors get caught in 'CHASING THE HOT DOT." This means looking for the best performing asset class in one year and putting all your dollars in that investment the next year. Outperformance of an asset class in one year doesn't mean repeat in the following year.

> *By properly diversifying a portfolio, investors can spread out their risk while also participating if one asset class performs well.*

No one can accurately and consistently predict when shifts in market leadership will occur or how long they will last. There are many asset classes including: paper assets, evergreen assets, real property and commodities to name a few. In the investment industry we concentrate on stocks, bonds and commodities. Most individual investors work with stocks and bonds. Diversification and asset allocation come from investing in large cap equities, small cap equities, domestic equities or foreign equities, etc.

Principle #5
True Diversification Reduces Potential Gains

If Investor A decides to invest his/her assets in large-cap growth equities exclusively, and it is the best performing asset class for a given period of time, that portfolio will grow accordingly and will outperform other asset classes.

However, as asset class leadership changes, Investor A is also exposing him/herself to a severe downtrend in large-cap growth. You give up some upside potential to protect yourself on the downside. Many investors learned the lesson of diversification during the late '90s during the "Tech Bubble." As the Dot-Com stocks took off, many investors who were diversified lagged behind the results of those investors who were over-weighted in tech stocks. Some of these diversified investors abandoned the asset allocation models and over-weighted in technology only to be destroyed when these high flyers crashed.

Principle #6:
Sell High and Buy Low

Conventional wisdom suggests "buy low and sell high." Conversely, our philosophy of selling high and buying low addresses the practice of effectively rebalancing diversified portfolios.

According to *Principles #4 and #5* investors should consider diversifying their portfolios with a plan to systematically rebalance them. This doesn't mean trying to pick the next hot asset class; rather it refers to working with an advisor to identify the right number of asset classes to build the appropriately diversified portfolio.

Quarterly, semi-annually, or annually a portfolio must be rebalanced to reflect its original breakdown. This practice forces investors to sell their "winners" and buy the under-performers. (Investors often have a very difficult time staying disciplined to this practice.)

History shows us that very rarely do asset classes repeat as the top performer from year to year. More importantly, rebalancing helps to prevent a portfolio from becoming over-weighted in a particular asset class. Some investors use the "dollar cost averaging" method of putting a certain amount each month or quarter into a particular mutual fund. Without knowing it, many investors are using the "dollar cost averaging" method when participating in their companies' 401k plan. But many investors do not take advantage of rebalancing to keep portfolios from being over-weighted in a particular sector. If an investor is disciplined "rebalancing" forces you to sell winners and buy the under performers. This protects you from getting hit hard when your over-weighted sector gets slammed.

Principle #7:

Invest All You Can with Before-Tax Dollars and/or in a Tax-Deferred Vehicle

Take full advantage of 401(k) plans, IRAs, and other tax-deferred vehicles. Money grows significantly faster in tax-deferred investments. Many investors know the great powers of compounding interest. In a tax deferred account, compounding, which some have labeled the 8th wonder of the world, becomes even more powerful.

> *For example, suppose investors contribute $10,000 to their IRA and decide to invest an additional $10,000 outside of their IRA in a taxable account. If both accounts grow by 10% in the first year, the IRA account value will be $11,000 while the taxable account will be worth only $10,700 ($11,000 − investors' 30% tax bracket).*

COACHING UP

Over time, because the investments have the opportunity to grow tax-deferred and the investors have been able to take full advantage of compounding interest, their portfolio will positively reflect their investment decision. It is also important to examine and understand how making pre-tax contributions to a qualified plan can reduce your taxable income.

Principle #8
Regression to the Mean

Each asset class has a very long history and can be analyzed to determine its historical return.

> *For example, the Dow Jones Industrial Average (DJIA) has averaged approximately a 10% return for the last 60 years. An investor must understand that a 20% return on the DJIA is atypical. Over time the average will return to the mean or in this case back to 10%.*

Investors must be careful not to chase the "hot" stock or asset class and be disciplined enough to properly diversify and rebalance their portfolios. These practices will help investors take advantage of the "regression to the mean" and not be hurt by their investment choices. A popular investment strategy called The

"Dogs of the Dow" takes advantage of the regression to the mean. Each year the dog's strategy invests in the top 10 highest yielding stocks in the Dow Jones average. The theory is because of their higher yields these stocks must be the worst-performing stocks in the Dow. If you believe in the regression to the mean these 10 stocks will outperform the next year. The next year you sell the shares and buy the 10 highest yielding stocks in the Dow.

Principle #9

An Investment Decision is a Good One if you know the "Risk and Reward"

When investors are faced with investment decisions they must determine if the true risk and the potential rewards are appropriate for them. Investors must find the proper balance between the two, which will help them weigh each investment opportunity to ensure that it fits within their overall plan. One cannot guarantee the performance of an investment, but an investment can be labeled a "Good One" if you know risk and that matches up with what you want.

> *Remember that there is no guarantee investments will perform as expected, but knowing the potential risks and reward involved give you the best opportunity to invest and succeed.*

Principle #10

When traveling through the Investment Forest you will encounter:

- **Many Trees (many investment opportunities)**
- **Trees of all sizes (large brokerage houses, small advisor firms)**
- **Constantly changing weather (changing interest rates, stock market up/down, economy robust or recession)**
- **A lot of wind (many financial professionals)**

If you are a financial professional these 10 principles can help you develop a great presentation, especially to retirees or soon-to-be-retired investors. If you are an investor, especially a new one, these principles may help you make those tough decisions.

CHAPTER 6

Advisory Account Quarterly Performance Reports: Advisors & Investors Must Use Them

Each quarter investors should receive quarterly performance reports from their advisor. Most of these reports are full of colorful bar charts and pie charts to make the reports easy on the eyes. Many investors get intimidated by the numbers and the number of pages. As an example, for an account with $250,000 in assets made up of a diversified portfolio of equities the report may contain twenty-one pages. These twenty-one pages are broken down as follows: one Title page, five pages of market analysis (economy, overall market and some thoughts going forward), five pages of performance numbers (the meat of the report), seven pages of holdings in the account, one page of fees charged, and two pages of disclosures. The twenty-one pages can make an investor put the report in a desk drawer to read later. There are really only six pages an investor has to look at and digest. These pages are the five pages of performance numbers and the one page of fee disclosures. Many investors don't take the time to digest the report so they can call their advisor to ask questions or be

ADVISORY ACCOUNT QUARTERLY PERFORMANCE REPORTS

prepared to discuss the report when/or if the advisor gives the investor a quarterly call. Every investor should definitely go over the 1st quarterly performance with their advisor. Ask your advisor to take some time to explain the 1st report.

If you haven't received performance reports prepared by a third-party analyst you definitely should get it from your advisor. If you haven't received your quarterly performance reports by the end of the month following the quarter's end (April 30th, July 31st, Oct. 31st, Jan. 31st) that should be a "red flag" to QUESTION your current advisor. What are my results? How am I doing? When and if you receive the performance reports, here is what to look for in those reports. Those six pages, the "meat" of the report:

1. We all start with the raw numbers: Is the dollar value of my account up or down, for the quarter, year to date, and since inception (when the advisor began to manage the assets)?
2. How has my investment done vs the benchmarks? A benchmark is an index that should closely mirror your risk tolerance and asset allocation? After looking at results vs the benchmark, ask your advisor why this particular benchmark is being used. Does it truly reflect your asset allocation and risk tolerance?
3. Check for any withdrawals to make sure you are aware of them all. Especially look for fees taken out and take the opportunity to evaluate these fees versus performance and advice. Does the quality of the performance and the quality of advice warrant fees paid? Does your advisor bring value? **Price is an issue in the absence of value.**
4. Check for the number of trades. You may want to question the advisor on trades to have the advisor articulate his/her strategies. An advisor's strategy is very important. If an advisor states that they are a growth manager, ask them how a particular trade fits the strategy. Pick out a particular trade

and ask WHY? What research did you do? Look at the pretty pie charts and ask why the current asset allocation (stocks, bonds, cash) or the current sector allocation (consumer, utilities, defense etc). If there are no trades you can still ask why. The number of trades in a fee based account has become an issue as many wire houses have responded to the proposed DOL Fiduciary law by putting all retirement accounts under a fee-based arrangement. When checking the number of trades, ask the question, "Would it have been cheaper to have paid commissions for those trades rather than a fee?" If commission trades continue to be cheaper than fees over a number of quarters it would be time to think about changing your fee-based account to a commission account. Make sure your advisor can justify all trades or lack of trades. But remember, you are paying a fee for advice and that advice may be to hold on to your current positions. You are paying for that advice.

5. Is your advisor using margin (borrowing money to buy more securities)? Make sure you understand margin because margin can put additional risk on your performance. You have to pay for funds borrowed. Ask your advisor how much you are paying on borrowed funds. Most firms charge a monthly interest rate on funds borrowed and deduct dollars owed monthly. These payments can reduce performance. In down markets this margin (leverage) can increase losses. As an example, let's look at one trade done using margin. We buy 1000 shares of XYZ that trades at $25/shr. The total trade is $25,000. We pay $15,000 and borrow $10,000. You have 60% equity in the trade and you are paying interest on the $10,000. Most institutions require equity to remain above 30% (can be changed by the institution at any time). If the market turns against the trade and XYZ goes down to $12/shr you now have 17% equity and you will get a margin call. Your advisor has to make a choice: sell enough shares to get your equity over 30% (forced sell), sell all your XYZ shares, bring in more money to

ADVISORY ACCOUNT QUARTERLY PERFORMANCE REPORTS

pay down margin amount (above 30%) and in a portfolio sell other company shares to raise cash. The major problem is that your advisor is making sell decisions based on margin calls, not strategy. Some advisors use margin to increase assets under management, thus increasing the fees they charge. Using the same numbers above you are paying fees on $25,000, not $15,000. That is a 60% increase in your fees. Check out margin balances.

6. Ask who generates these reports. If they are not generated by someone other than the advisor, ask why not. A report generated by a third party gives the investor more faith that the numbers are correct.

A quarterly performance report is a powerful tool for investors to evaluate their financial advisor. Don't be intimidated by the numbers or the number of pages. Go to the meat of the report and get the important questions answered.

CHAPTER 7

Leadership

I don't motivate the players. I get them to motivate themselves. That's the only kind of motivation that's worth a damn. -*Woody Hayes*

You eliminate those who are not motivated.
                                        -Lou Holtz

1. 10/80/10
2. 80/20
3. AxV=G
4. Red Zone
5. LQERT
6. Develop Strengths, Overcome Weaknesses Based on the Uncomfortable
7. Coach Up
8. Magic Formula for Winning
9. Know Superstar Traits
10. Can't Make Everybody Happy/Take One Off Your Chest
11. Progress is Change in the Direction You Think Change Should Be
12. Take Care of the Little Things
13. Manage By Walking Around (MBWA)

Thoughts About Leadership
10/80/10 Rule

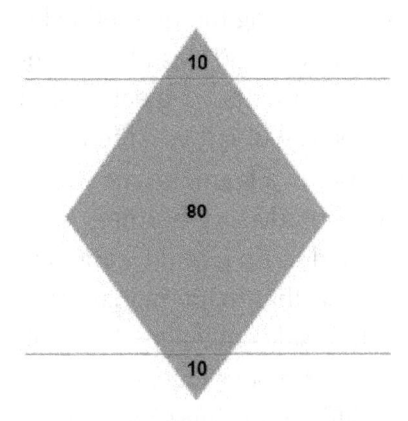

This rule and how a leader handles it could be the most important determination of a leader's success. The diamond-shaped figure represents the total participants that fall under a leader's watch. The diamond-shaped figure could be a team, an office, a classroom or a company. I have found that no matter how small or how large the group is, the 10/80/10 rule works. The upper 10% represents the group of associates who are now or are close to being "superstars." The main function of the leader when working with this group is to make sure you do not screw them up. See what they need, listen to them, make sure they know you appreciate them. Because a leader may not want to take a chance in "screwing them up," some leaders make the mistake of not spending time with them. Make sure you spend some time and again make sure they know you appreciate them. Also, connecting the top ten to the bottom ten in order to mentor may be helpful to those that are "coachable."

The large 80% group is the group with which the leader has to work. Coach them up, base your training modules on this group. Make them better, hopefully some can move into the upper 10%. Award programs, sales meetings, and tracking programs must be directed to this group. Much of a leader's time is spent with this group. Many leaders will spend most of their time with the upper 10%, because it's fun and there are very few headaches. These are superstars. To use a football analogy, the upper 10% is like coaching the quarterbacks: fun easy and very little dirt. Coaching the middle 80% is like coaching the linemen. It is hard, it is dirty and doesn't get a great deal of attention. Any head coach of a football team will tell you the offensive and defensive line coaches make or break a team. I have always personally worked with new trainees in the advisory business for a number of reasons. First, I have been trained to do it and I want new advisors to do it the right way. You will find that many managers in the advisory business relegate this duty to a sales manager. I do not. Second, it helps me build loyalty to the firm and our office. If a trainee feels you helped them make it in a very difficult business they have a loyalty that becomes important when they begin to get those recruiting calls. Yes — you cannot "outsource" relationships. The highest form of leadership is by example. The lowest form of leadership is positioning: "me the boss, you the subordinate."

The bottom 10% of the diamond is the group that more often than not will make or break the success of an office, a team, or a company. How well a leader handles this group determines the team's success and the leader's success. The main goal of a leader is to make sure this lower 10% group doesn't take control of the total group–especially the 80% group. It is very easy just to eliminate this group; sometimes if you want to change your people, you have to "change your people." But in some cases, not so easy. In the brokerage/advisory business it is not easy to get rid of a top producer who is living on the compliance edge. In the sports world it is not easy to get rid of the talented receiver who comes late to practice and doesn't like practicing. Both types of individuals can hurt your office or your team.

Of course, your first step is to try to coach up your lower 10%'ers. But if you have put them in the lower 10%, the idea of coaching them up has already been determined. They must be eliminated. Lose some points, lose some production but do what is right for the team, the clients and you. The key is that a successful leader must determine who the bottom 10% are and not let them gain control of your office or your locker room.

80/20 rule

The 80/20 rule is a very well known rule that normally means that 80% of an advisor's production comes from 20% of the clients. It is imperative that advisors who are trying to grow and develop their practices understand this rule and use it to help grow their practices. It was quite enjoyable to watch experienced advisors who came through our business development programs squirm uncomfortably when the program started off by highlighting the 80/20 rule and the need to get rid of low-producing, time-consuming clients. No advisor likes to give up any clients. At least one advisor in any group would lament that one of these low-producing clients might come into a large inheritance or win the lottery. My response: you have a client on the books who has not done any business with you in two years and when they get a large sum of money to invest they are going to work with you. After getting through the awkward, but necessary discussions on eliminating wasted energy and time, the main thrust of the development programs was to refine your "must prospecting discipline" and segment your clients and leads to better service clients and better prospect existing lead sources. Client segmentation is done through setting up a grading system and using that grading system to put clients into categories. I have seen advisors use "platinum, gold, silver" or a simple "a, b, c." These client groupings are based on production, assets, whether easy/hard to work with, referral source and any other criteria an advisor sees fit. Each advisor then has to determine what services and benefits each category receives. Client segmentation is relatively easy; the prospecting leads segmentation is more difficult. Many advisors don't see the **80/20 rule** relating to prospecting. Most advisors have a large list of leads and this list sits in a file drawer gathering dust because they don't have a plan to work the list. Many advisors are emboldened once they try this exercise. To be a successful prospector or gatherer of assets, we have to get the list on paper so that we can develop clever and unique ways of approaching these leads. Prospecting leads are tagged based on eagerness, motivation, level of engagement and interest in your practice. Asset level is not the main criteria. Unearth all contacts, and I mean all, from scattered repositories. These contacts should include, but not be limited to, prospects, friends, family, acquaintances, in-laws, outlaws, creditors, debtors. Use all scattered repositories such as cell phone, rolodex, envelopes, bar napkins, business cards, holiday lists, club directories, alumni, google contacts, linked-in, Facebook. Import this list to a spreadsheet with a, b, c, d tabs.

A prospects: have the need, are qualified to buy, and are sincerely interested in making a decision soon. You review this tab once a day.

B prospects: apparently qualified, have the need, but are not highly motivated. They're waiting for some future event to make them **a.** Review this tab once a week

C prospects: are any prospects who cannot be classified as **a** or **b**. Review this tab once a month.

D prospects: "orphans" that is, former clients from your current and prior occupation

You are constantly upgrading this list, adding names, moving names from tab to tab. These are lists for seminars, monthly newsletters, analyst reports, etc.

This is the blueprint for a sales pipeline, creating your business success. It beats waiting for the phone to ring.

A x V=G

As I have stated before, all great leaders believe strongly in how to grow the business, how to win. It makes decisions easier whether they be spending capital, training, or hiring. As leaders explain their philosophy to associates the decisions made can be better understood by all. I believe the path to success in the advisory business revolves around the formula **A x V=G.** The formula simply stated means that the (A) assets under management, times the (V) velocity we turn, those assets will equal (G) gross production. In today's regulatory environment, plus the extremely competitive industry we cannot rely on increasing velocity, we must increase A to increase our revenue. Fees and commissions are being compressed. Our velocity rates are on average 1%. Long gone are the 2%-3% days.

If we must increase A then all business decisions must be made to meet the increase A goal. Our hiring is made easier because we are looking for relationship builders who can bring in more assets. We are looking for advisors who understand they must develop a "must prospecting discipline." We must help advisors with the training and the tools to gather more assets. Spending capital decisions are made easier: if it doesn't help bring in assets we don't invest.

One great leader who personified the strong belief leadership style was Woody Hayes, the great successful coach at Ohio State. Coach Hayes believed in a strong running attack with the pass being a secondary weapon. He recruited players that fit into the "three yards and a cloud of dust" mentality. He spent money on weight rooms that helped make his players stronger and faster. Many detractors downplayed his style but he believed in it. He made all decisions based on his belief and all he did was win.

Strong beliefs in how the industry works or how the game is played can help a leader become successful.

COACHING UP

Successful advisors score in the red zone

In football the red zone is defined as the twenty yards before your goal line. Great football teams score when they get into the red zone on a consistent basis. When you line up in the red zone the game changes. The field is compressed to thirty yards (twenty yards plus ten yards in the end zone. Defenses line up in tougher defenses. It becomes a battle between individual players. No fancy plays. Just player on player.

In the brokerage/advisory business the "red zone" is the closing of the sale. No fancy brochures, no videos--just the advisor closing. Many unsuccessful advisors would rather talk about the markets, interest rates or tax rates but that doesn't work when it is time to close. This is no different than many other industries when the closing red zone is in play. Great closers succeed. As a leader you must be able to coach up advisors on how to win in the red zone. Sales meetings are littered with great brochures on products, great videos on the economy, but not many concentrate on scoring in the red zone. Get tougher, ask for the order, handle the objections.

HANDLING OBJECTIONS (LQERT) no objections means they're not listening or not qualified, and consequently won't buy — they announce their intention and point the way to closing. Prospects wouldn't keep talking (objecting) if they didn't want to place money with you. Objections are concerns and until you learn how to handle them you'll never reach potential; champion salespeople have an affection for objections because it's something concrete!

Objections tell you interests and reveal what you are to emphasize, eliminate, or change before closing. There are three types:

1. <u>Minor</u> objections (delay tactic) — buyers' reflexes for slowing down the process...they don't even realize they come out as objections: eg: we only see vendors on Tuesday; we're only

looking, think it over, call me in a month, we're already using someone. You don't have to address all minor objections!
2. <u>Majors</u>: your product or service has perceived limits and thus, a prospect cannot see how it fulfills needs.
3. <u>Conditions</u>: block the sale and cannot be overcome; it's a valid reason for not going ahead.

For many years I have used the LGERT method to handle objections. Someone told me it was originally developed in the IBM training classes. It has proven very helpful in handling objections.

(l) listen to the objection, make sure your prospective client can see you are listening.

(q) question to clarify, to make sure you handle the correct objection. Questioning helps you show that you are listening and by questioning it may give you time to formulate your response. As an advisor brand new in the business I learned to use questions to clarify after handling objections that didn't exist. I was talking to a client about purchasing 1000 shares of Ohio Edison. After I stopped talking, the client asked, "Does Ohio Edison have nuclear power?" I immediately went into all problems of nuclear power but Ohio Edison could handle any of those problems. The client said she would have to think about it because she'd never thought about the nuclear problems. If I had asked "Why do you ask?" or "Does something concern you about nuclear power plants?" I would have learned that the client had heard that utilities pay a higher dividend and she just wanted to know. So I answered the wrong objection. In sales, assumption is the mother of all screw-ups. And I lost the sale. Another reason to question is that you get a chance to show the prospect that you are listening. And the final reason to question is to have time to think about your response.

(e) empathize. "I see where you are coming from," or "Many of my clients have had that concern."

(r) respond with your answer to the question

(t) test for acceptance. You are asking whether they can agree or at least see where you are coming from. Don't move on unless you're sure you have handled the objection.

When you get the acceptance, close again......

Identify the strengths and weaknesses of your associates

Great leaders identify the strengths and weaknesses of all their associates. Work with each advisor to develop the advisor's strengths. It has always been an important part of a leader's mandate to identify strengths of their advisors. Working with advisors to develop these strengths can help a team or office succeed. I believe it is just as important for a leader to identify weaknesses and help overcome those weaknesses. Most weaknesses can be identified by asking a simple question: "What activity makes you uncomfortable?" Many advisors hit a production plateau and have difficulty breaking through to the next level. When I am working with an advisor who wants to get to the next production level which really means increase assets under management, I ask the question: "What activity in this business makes you uncomfortable?" It is very important to identify the "uncomfortable" because I have always believed **successful advisors do the uncomfortable activities that the unsuccessful advisors don't or won't do**. The new advisors and some experienced advisors are uncomfortable prospecting, whether it be cold calling, seminars, networking and, with experienced advisors, asking their client base for referrals. After identifying the weaknesses or uncomfortable activity, the leader must develop a plan to overcome the weaknesses. Make the advisor comfortable and success follows.

LEADERSHIP

Coach up

Coaching up (vs coaching down) helps when a leader wants to assist an advisor to overcome weaknesses. As an example, an advisor comes into a quarterly planning meeting and expresses the frustration of not being able to break through a production plateau. "Coaching down" leaders would do a few things. They would take out the numbers that probably show not enough outgoing calls, not enough new account openings and, of course, very little increase in assets under management. The "coaching down" leader would concentrate on the negatives. When an advisor is looking to break through a production plateau in trying to coach up, instead of concentrating on those negatives , I always ask: "What activity makes you uncomfortable?" because I know if the advisor identifies his/her weakness they are more likely to buy into overcoming that weakness (beat the activity that makes them uncomfortable). If asking for referrals makes them uncomfortable, help them develop a better "must prospecting discipline," that is, show them how to ask for referrals, I don't believe that anyone has to be torn down and then built back up.

Magic formula for winning

I have used this "magic formula for winning" for 20+ years. I am not sure where I got it but I love it.

Magic formula for winning

1. **You beat 50% of the people in America by working <u>hard</u>.**
2. **You beat 40% by being a person of honesty, integrity and standing <u>for</u> something.**
3. **10% is a *DOGFIGHT!***

Traits of a superstar advisor

I have developed this list of the characteristics that many superstars in the advisory/brokerage business demonstrate. It was developed with the cooperation of many attendees to training sessions in which I had participated. I simply asked the question: "Tell me what you see when you are watching the "big producers" in your office."

The 12 dimensions of a superstar

1. **Confidence:** A trusting or reliance; an assurance of mind or firm belief in the integrity, stability or veracity of another, or in the truth and reality of a fact.
2. **Hard Work:** to be in motion without yielding to pressure.
3. **Positive Mental Attitude**
4. **Goal Oriented/Focused**
5. **Disciplined:** to prepare by instructing in correct principles and habits
6. **Persistent:** continuing without withering
7. **Demonstrating Conviction**
8. **Competitive**
9. **Exhibiting ability to Sell**
10. Coachable
11. Knowledgeable
12. Using Professionalism

I have listed all the positive traits. I usually finish the discussion by asking about any negative observations. The biggest observation is that some superstars can be jerks. This allows me to talk about not being abusive to the staff, other advisors, wholesalers and, of course, management. If a leader is working to develop the advisors, they are appreciated. The above list is a great help when you are hiring or recruiting.

Can't make everyone happy; may have to take one off the chest

When I was playing college baseball I remember something a coach once said about playing third base. You may have to take a ground ball off your chest. It sometimes surprises me when leaders avoid making tough decisions because that is when a leader must take one off the chest. It is going to hurt, it is going to be uncomfortable, and someone usually will not be happy. When a leader has strong beliefs about the way the business operates, these tough, uncomfortable decisions can be a little easier. But at the end of the day great leaders make the tough decisions, knowing you can't make everyone happy and it will hurt.

Progress is change in the direction you think change should be

A great leader knows that all decisions will not be accepted by everyone. All the advisors may not agree upon a leader's definition of progress. When presenting a new idea, a new product or a new policy, leaders must anticipate that there will be questions and concerns. Be prepared to handle objections and concerns. Great leaders understand in advance that everyone in the group may not see this as progress. One of the hardest changes to implement is a philosophy change. The best example in the brokerage/advisory business is the philosophy change from commission business to fee-based business. Experienced brokers were asked to change their core businesses. It took many years for the concept of SMA accounts to take hold. It was definitely progress, but many brokers didn't like or accept the direction of this change. The successful leaders anticipated the objections and stayed the course even it didn't make everyone happy.

Take care of the little things

When I was coaching college football I spent a week at North Carolina State's spring practice. The head coach at the time was the legendary Lou Holtz. When we were preparing to leave, Coach Holtz invited me into his office and asked me what were some of the things I had learned. I proceeded to talk about the offensive and defensive schemes I had learned. I also mentioned the coaching techniques that were used by his assistants. We discussed what I had mentioned and then before I left he told me: "If you want to be a successful coach make sure you **take care of the little things."** This statement has stuck with me for many years. One recent example that comes to mind is a little thing that cost us some production. An advisor was upset about some policy changes in the office and was deciding whether he should leave or not. After many hours of discussion he blurted out that we didn't want to help him grow his business. This surprised me because we pride ourselves in helping advisors get to the next level. I asked him to give me an example that proves we do not want to work with him. He told me that our chief compliance officer kept her office lights off (she later said the lights gave her a headache). He interpreted that to mean she kept the lights off because she didn't want anyone to bother her. He was offended. Talk about little things! But if we pride ourselves in helping our advisors, lights off don't project the image we want. Needless to say, all our leadership team have their lights on. Take care of the little things with anticipation.

Manage by walking around (MBWA)

Leaders do not hide behind closed doors with lights off. Great leaders get out with the troops. Force yourself every day to walk around the office. Talk about the markets, talk about politics, talk about families. Listen more than you speak. You may find out some little problems that could fester into bigger problems. *Motivation is simple.*

CHAPTER 8

A New Mandate for Financial Advisors

Financial advisors have helped clients meet financial goals and objectives. Advisors help clients retire in comfort, help put kids through college, or work to increase income for retirees. A new mandate has appeared that has put another burden on financial advisors. Most retail investors get their information from what many call the "main street media" (MSM). Investors read local papers to see what happened in the markets. Especially in times when the markets are moving in extremes, either up or down, retail investors rely on what they read in the paper, see on the nightly news or look up on the internet. I am convinced that the financial "main street media" (I include large "wire house" research departments in this observation), are biased by anti-Trump sentiment that makes financial market stories very misleading. I have been watching the financial press for many years. Since the 2015 primaries it has become very obvious to me that the MSM financial press suffers from the Trump derangement syndrome.

Each morning I send out a short email newsletter to advisors that we hope helps the advisors answer questions from their clients. This email newsletter is a way for me to help them get an immediate idea or gauge of what happened overnight and what is happening in the morning. In preparation to write this daily newsletter (haven't missed a day in ten years), I go over local and national financial news articles to see what will help advisors and their clients make the best investment decisions. I can say with certainty that the "main street media" has a distinct dislike for President Trump and will do or write anything to make him look bad. In my opinion they will slant, mislead, or omit news even if it hurts the economy, the stock market and investors. The mantra for most media outlets is "bad press is good copy." Media Trump Hatred Shows in 92% Negative Coverage of his Presidency: Investors' Business Daily Study 10/18/2018.

Let's start with the financial press pre-election, 2016. Remember I am hoping to help advisors assist clients who mostly are not in the financial industry. These clients rely on the "main street media" for news. Donald Trump is a businessman, pro- business, less regulations and is running on making the American economy better. Here is what clients were reading and hearing that could affect their investment decisions. I wish we could find out the number of 401k participants who moved money into cash pre-2016 election because they feared a Trump presidency. They would have missed out on a great ride through the end of 2017 alone. Since the day Donald Trump was elected president in November 2016, the Dow Jones Industrial average rose by apprx. 35% through December 2017. These results reflected one of the greatest 14-month period bull-market runs in history. Who can blame these do-it-yourselfers if they were getting their financial news from the main street media? Just look at what these investors were reading and hearing in the main street financial press.

"Donald Trump's first gift to the world will be another financial crisis." Headline in the U.K. Independent. *"(He) gives every impression that he will soon be hustling America — and possibly the entire world — in the direction of another catastrophic financial crisis."*

"It really does now look like President Donald J. Trump, and markets

A NEW MANDATE FOR FINANCIAL ADVISORS

are plunging. When might we expect them to recover? A first-pass answer is never... So we are very probably looking at a global recession, with no end in sight." Paul Krugman of the New York Times the day after the election.

"If Trump wins we should expect a big markdown in expected future earnings for a wide range of stocks — and a likely crash in the broader market." Eric Zitzewitz, former chief economist at the IMF, November 2016.

"Under Trump, I would expect a protracted recession to begin within 18 months. The damage would be felt far beyond the United States." Former Clinton and Obama chief economist Larry Summers, June 2016.

"Trump would likely cause the stock market to crash and plunge the world into recession." Simon Johnson, MIT economics professor, in The New York Times, November 2016.

"Citigroup: A Trump Victory in November Could Cause a Global Recession," Bloomberg Financial News headline, August 2016.

"I have never seen an election in which the markets have so strong of a view as to what was good and bad about the outcome. And what you saw was the markets rallying yesterday because of the FBI thing on Sunday. And the reason I mention this particularly is if the likely event happens and Trump wins, you will see a market crash of historic proportions, I think...The markets are terrified of him." Steve Rattner, MSNBC economics guru and former Obama Car Czar, October, 2016.

"Wall Street is set up for a major crash if Donald Trump shocks the world on Election Day and wins the White House. **New research** *out on Friday suggests that financial markets strongly prefer a Hillary Clinton presidency and could react with panicked selling should*

COACHING UP

Trump defy the polls and deliver a shocking upset on Nov. 8." Ben White, Politico, October 2016.

"A President Trump Could Destroy the World Economy," headline of Washington Post editorial, October 2016.

The chart below shows the negative bias to President Trump pre-election. Numbers don't lie.

<u>Newspaper endorsements in the 2016 United States presidential election</u>

Candidate	Daily	Weekly	Magazines	College	International	Total
Hillary Clinton	243	148	15	77	17	500
No endorsement	64	13	0	5	0	82
Not Donald Trump	8	2	4	12	4	30
Donald Trump	20	6	0	0	2	28
Gary Johnson	9	0	0	0	0	9
Split endorsement	2	0	0	0	0	2
Evan McMullin	1	0	0	0	0	1
Not Hillary Clinton	1	0	0	0	0	1

The Las Vegas Review-Journal was the only major newspaper in the nation to come out for Trump.*

*politico

If you had no one else to talk to and all your financial decisions were based on what you read or see in the financial news main street media, what would you do?

The financial MSM has not stopped their attacks even after Trump was elected. In fact, it has grown more biased, more misleading and frankly more untrue.

A NEW MANDATE FOR FINANCIAL ADVISORS

The day after the 2018 midterms the following was written in the Wall Street Journal:

"The Dow Jones Industrial Average surged nearly 550 points Wednesday as U.S. stocks extended a recent rebound, advancing as a congressional power divide eased worries about swift policy changes that could hurt large companies. Uncertainty about the elections was one factor driving October's stock-market rout, with some investors anxious that radical economic policy changes could hurt corporations benefiting from tax reform and an emphasis on deregulation. Democrats claiming a majority in the House of Representatives and Republicans retaining control of the Senate soothed some of those fears, analysts said, sparking a broad-based market rally."

The markets were down significantly pre-election and the financial press blamed Trump-induced trade wars, impending recession, Fed rate increases. Never, and I mean never, did I read: "Uncertainty about the elections was one factor driving October's stock-market rout, with some investors anxious that radical economic policy changes could hurt corporations benefiting from tax reform and an emphasis on deregulation. Pre-midterm elections, the financial press stayed away from mentioning anything about voters being worried about a Democratic sweep of both houses changing policies that would hurt the economy. If the MSM financial press had acknowledged that investors were worried about a Democratic sweep hurting the economy, thus being a possible reason for the October stock market downturn, they would have been helping Trump and the Republican party keep control of both houses. They omitted mention of investors' fears and concentrated on the fear of Trump tariff wars as reasons for the October market swoon. Blame Trump to keep him and the Republicans from complete control. They tried to help win the Senate also, but they failed.

Another added responsibility for financial advisors is reading the articles, not the headlines, so that they can give investors the true story. Take a look at a CNBC article headline dated December 27, 2018.

"Jobless claims signal labor market strength, consumer confidence tumbles"

The positive of "Labor market strength" is conveniently offset by "consumer confidence tumbles." When you read the article, way down in the middle of the paragraphs you read this:

"In a sign some consumers are worried about the economy, the Conference Board's consumer confidence index declined modestly in December,

Despite the drop, the index still pointed to solid economic growth in the short term, said Lynn Franco, senior director of economic indicators at the Conference Board."

Declined **"modestly"** is not "tumbles" and the index still points to **"solid economic growth."** This is a great example of the MSM trying to talk the U.S. economy into a recession and pushing the stock market lower. This is all done to harm Donald Trump, even if means harming U.S investors. The new mandate is that financial advisors must read and decipher false, misleading and just "fake news" for investors so the investors do not make decisions based on what they read in the MSM.

As the MSM tries to talk the economy into a recession they are using new tactics. CNBC will identify any commentator that is quoted with positive economic news as a Trump supporter. On January 22, 2018 this was written on the CNBC website: "Economic growth may be slowing, but we are not on the verge of a recession, Blackstone Chairman and CEO Steve Schwarzman said Tuesday. "The U.S.

A NEW MANDATE FOR FINANCIAL ADVISORS

economy is slowing from where it was. Two quarters ago, we were at 4.2 percent economic growth, which is unsustainable for a large country like the United States," Schwarzman told CNBC's "Squawk Box " at the annual World Economic Forum in Davos, Switzerland. "We'll probably grow at about 2.5 percent to 2.75 percent this year." However, "I don't see any recession. I don't know where that came from the last two months of the year. Consumer confidence is down a little bit, which I think comes from some of the dysfunction, but they are still spending a lot of money," Schwarzman said. However, "I don't see any recession. I don't know where that came from the last two months of the year. Consumer confidence is down a little bit, which I think comes from some of the dysfunction, but they are still spending a lot of money," Schwarzman concluded. A top GOP donor and close advisor to President Donald Trump

This gentleman is the CEO and chairman of Blackstone, an investment firm that has 457 billion in assets but CNBC feels the need to let readers know he backs Trump. WHY? I am still waiting to see the political leanings of anyone who predicts a recession. So far I haven't seen any.

Financial advisors are very much needed, more than ever. Do-it-yourselfers will be investing on "bad" information fostered by the MSM wanting to get rid of Trump and investors be "damned."

CHAPTER 9

Another Warning "Nobody Loses"

I must address another warning to all advisors and managers in the financial industry that concerns "protecting your franchise." There is a new group of investors, regulators and politicians who are starting to come into our industry or as politicians who have oversight on our industry. We can call them millennials or snowflakes but they must be dealt with. Caution is the key word when dealing with this group. This is a unique group who have grown up in an environment that makes it difficult to relate well to our industry. This group has been told that no one loses. They have played soccer games (no football, too risky), baseball games and many other games where no one is supposed to keep score. Everyone gets a reward (trophy) just for participating. Any risk of injury is avoided. This group did away with dodgeball. They have tried to eliminate the risk of "feeling bad." Too much success is frowned upon for fear it will hurt someone else's feelings. Many schools have eliminated the concept of valedictorian because someone who didn't get the award might feel bad. They shun the idea of rewarding hard work.

The term "safe space" has become a household word especially in our colleges.

In the schools the concept of capitalism is not presented in a positive way. Capitalism develops winners and losers; we can't have any losers! It comes as no great surprise that in a recent survey 44% of millennials like the idea of socialism.

Why do I warn you to be cautious about dealing with this group?

Snowflakes as clients. They do not understand risk. They have been sheltered from all kinds of risk and now they are investing. Everything they know says to avoid anything that has risk. They may nod their heads when you discuss risk, but do they really comprehend? You must take a great deal of time to explain risk. Risk cannot be avoided in our business. Some might say that if you keep all your money in cash there is no risk. Of course, these risk avoiders have inflation risk and buying power risk. You may not be able to get "snowflakes" to invest in anything that has any smell of risk, but you better make sure they understand the inherent risks because when they don't have the retirement funds to retire comfortably they will be looking for answers. Why don't I get a trophy?

If you give these millennials a financial plan that includes stocks and bonds that they accept, make sure they can accept losing. Remember they have been told that there are no losers; if you participate you are a winner. I can hear the litigation complaints about not understanding risk, not being told about the risk and "I deserve to win."

Also, when you start working with the "snowflake" generation you have to educate them about the basic concepts of capitalism. Make sure you know the term "sustainable." This group has been brought up with the term and, frankly, they embrace sustainable everything. Take a look at the proliferation of mutual funds investing in sustainable companies. Remember they have been schooled that capitalism has many downsides and that socialism may be the answer.

"Snowflakes as regulators" As this group infiltrates the ranks of regulators, make sure you understand that when you are working with "snowflake" regulators they don't like you because you represent capitalism. They have come into this position to protect investors from you, capitalists, who have succeeded at the expense of others. This is what they have been told. You make too much money. Two examples will illustrate my warning. During a recent SEC audit I was sitting in a meeting with three SEC regulators whose ages were not above thirty, in my opinion. They were looking at my personal banking statement when one of the "snowflakes" asked, "What is this check made out to FORD?" I explained that it was for a car payment. The "snowflake" SEC regulator replied snarkily, "Did you sell your Mercedes?" My interpretation was that he was saying: "You advisors make too much money."

The recent Labor Department's Fiduciary Rule fiasco is a great example of the "snowflake" mentality taking over the decisions made at the Labor Department. First of all, the Labor Department has no business sticking their nose into financial matters. They came up with this plan predicated on a false narrative that IRA investors lose money working with advisors. They came up with a plan that did nothing but hurt small IRA investors who because of this plan would not be serviced. The "snowflake" regulators were more concerned about hurting the advisors' pocketbooks than helping IRA investors save for retirement.

"Snowflakes as politicians" As this group gets involved in our political system, the call for the dismantling of our capitalistic economy will become more intense. As we try to build portfolios we must research companies with not only good profits but also sustainable ones. And evaluate the corporations which work for "social justice." Remember there cannot be 'winners and losers." The previously discussed Labor Department Fiduciary Rule will become commonplace as politicians overreach their authorities in the name of "fairness for all." Advisors may have to lead the fight to stop the "snowflakes" from eroding our great economic system, CAPITALISM, that has made the USA the greatest country in the world.

The "snowflake" generation and their enablers have to accept the fact that if you invest in stocks and bonds not everyone gets a trophy and we do keep score.